W9-BDK-935

First edition for the United States and Canada published
in 2010 by Barron's Educational Series, Inc.

First edition of *Why do I feel scared?*
first published in 2010 by Wayland, a division of Hachette Children's Books

All inquiries should be addressed to:
Barron's Educational Series, Inc.
250 Wireless Boulevard
Hauppauge, NY 11788
www.barronseduc.com

Library of Congress Control No.: 2010923340

ISBN-13: 978-0-7641-4514-8
ISBN-10: 0-7641-4514-2

Printed in China
9 8 7 6 5 4 3 2 1

Manufactured by: Shenzhen Wing King Tong Paper Products Co. Ltd., Shenzhen, Guangdong, China.
May 2010

Why do I feel scared?

A FIRST LOOK AT BEING BRAVE

PAT THOMAS
ILLUSTRATED BY LESLEY HARKER

BARRON'S

The world is full of brave people.

But sometimes the bravest people aren't always the ones we think they are.

Bravery and courage are special gifts.
But they are not something you are born with.

They are choices you make in your heart.

What about you?

Can you think of some brave people you know?

What sorts of things have they done?

There are lots of ways
of being brave.

And not all of them are big and noisy like
in the movies or on TV.

People become brave when they act in a certain way—

such as when they tell the truth, even when other
people don't want to hear it.

Or when they keep trying,
even if they are not very
good at something,
or it is hard...

...or they probably
won't win a prize.

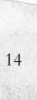

People are brave when they are willing to be themselves, even if it means being a little different...

...and when they stand up for others who find it hard to stand up for themselves.

Brave people always ask themselves what the right thing to do is—and then that is what they do.

What about you?

Have you ever done anything brave? Can you think of a time when you kept trying even when it was hard?

Being brave doesn't mean
you are never afraid.

In fact, sometimes if you
are afraid there is a good reason.

People who dare you
to do something scary
that is wrong are not
good friends.

18

They will lead you into trouble.

But sometimes the things we are afraid of seem scary just because they are new, or different, or difficult...

20

...or because we imagine they are
more scary than they really are.

21

Being brave is a lot like
many things we do every day.

Some days it's easy and some days it's hard.

But you have to practice in order to get good at it.

And the more you practice,
the easier it gets.

The world needs a lot
more brave people.

Do you think you could
be one of them?

HOW TO USE THIS BOOK

Courage is an important capacity for children to develop. Courage is daring to do what's right when that feels uncomfortable, scary, or dangerous. It is learned through daily experience, through how people act, and through what they say.

When you help children develop courage you encourage them in many important ways. You help them develop the power to say no to others who are urging them to join in harmful or destructive behaviors. You help them learn to stand up and protect others who are weaker than they are. And you instill in them the confidence to try new things and to be true to themselves.

Like all aspects of parenting, courage is a lesson best learned in an atmosphere of acceptance and respect. If a child feels safe enough to express his or her fears it will be much easier to explore and eventually outgrow or overcome those fears. As a parent it is important to recognize that all fears—big and small—are real to children. They need to be taken seriously, not punished, or ridiculed or worse ignored.

Some fears are legitimate and age appropriate. Toddlers, for instance, may fear separation from parents, strangers and other unknown things. As a child matures so does his or her imagination and it is not unusual for pre-schoolers and school age children to fear the dark, being left alone, strange animals, being injured or dying and other situations over which they feel they have little control.

A consistent daily routine, where the child knows what to expect, can help with this and can provide children with a sense of power and control.

It is important to recognize your child's moments of personal courage and praise the child. It's all too easy, from an adult perspective, to forget how much courage it sometimes takes for kids to do little things. Encouragement and praise from you when your child makes it to the top of the monkey bars, or makes a new friend are very important in helping your child feel safe enough to continue exploring new territory.

Make sure you share your own acts of courage with your children. Don't wait for some big moment of bravery that you can weave into an entertaining tale. Most of us have to do little courageous things every day whether it is meeting the new boss or speaking up when we see something that is wrong.

Schools can help foster courage by helping children explore the concept in both abstract and practical ways. By using examples from history, teachers can introduce the subject of courage. The life stories of others who have faced fear, such as Anne Frank or Helen Keller, can be inspirational as well as help to give history a human face. Story time can feature entertaining stories of courage (e.g. *The Wizard of Oz* or *Babe*) and there is a wealth of children's fiction to choose from in this regard.

Group discussions can ask such questions as "What is courage?" "Can you think of some examples of courage that you have seen or heard about?" "Does being brave always mean taking risks? Why or why not." Children can be encouraged to talk or write about times they have faced a challenge that required them to be brave, and to express the feeling of that experience and how they overcame their fears.

For parents, too, reading to your children is a good way to stimulate thoughts and conversations. There are many children's fiction books that tell tales of courage. What children feel about these stories is often quite revealing. Find ways to weave the themes of those stories into your daily conversations.

BOOKS TO READ

Babe the Gallant Pig
Dick King Smith (Dell, 1988)

Island of the Blue Dolphins
Scott O'Dell (Yearling Books, 1987)

The Wonderful Wizard of Oz
Frank Baum (Oxford Children's Classics, 2008)

Heroic Stories
Anthony Masters (Kingfisher Books, 1994)

What Do You Think? A Kids Guide to Dealing with Daily Dilemmas
Linda Schwartz (Learning Works, 1991)

The Children's Book of Virtues
William J. Bennett (Simon & Schuster, 1996)

Kids with Courage: True Stories About Young People Making a Difference
Barbara A. Lewis (Free Spirit Publishing, 1992)

Teaspoon of Courage for Kids: A Little Book of Encouragement for Whenever You Need It
Bradley Trevor Grieve (Andrews McNeel Publishing, 2007)

RESOURCES FOR ADULTS

The Values Book: Teaching Sixteen Basic Values to Young Children
Pam Schiller, Tamera Bryant (Gryphon House, 1998)

Teaching Your Children Values
Linda and Richard Eyre (Fireside, 1993)

The Book of Virtues: A Treasury of Great Moral Stories
William J. Bennett (Simon & Schuster, 1993)

What Do You Stand For?
Barbara A. Lewis (Free Spirit, 1998)